MY SENSES

Touch

LET'S READ
AV²
BY WEIGL™
ADDED VALUE • AUDIO VISUAL

Go to **www.av2books.com**, and enter this book's unique code.

BOOK CODE

G19061

AV² by Weigl brings you media enhanced books that support active learning.

AV² provides enriched content that supplements and complements this book. Weigl's AV² books strive to create inspired learning and engage young minds in a total learning experience.

Your AV² Media Enhanced books come alive with...

Audio
Listen to sections of the book read aloud.

Video
Watch informative video clips.

Embedded Weblinks
Gain additional information for research.

Try This!
Complete activities and hands-on experiments.

Key Words
Study vocabulary, and complete a matching word activity.

Quizzes
Test your knowledge.

Slide Show
View images and captions, and prepare a presentation.

... and much, much more!

Published by AV² by Weigl
350 5th Avenue, 59th Floor New York, NY 10118
Website: www.av2books.com   www.weigl.com

Durrie, Karen.
Touch / Karen Durrie.
     p. cm. -- (My senses)
 Includes bibliographical references and index.
 ISBN 978-1-61913-313-6 (hard cover : alk. paper) -- ISBN 978-1-61913-318-1 (soft cover : alk. paper)
1. Touch--Juvenile literature. I. Title.
 QP451.D87 2013
 612.8'8--dc23
                              2012000209

Printed in the United States of America in North Mankato, Minnesota
1 2 3 4 5 6 7 8 9 0   16 15 14 13 12

062012
WEP050412
Project Coordinator: Aaron Carr   Design: Mandy Christiansen

Weigl acknowledges Getty Images, iStock, and Dreamstime as image suppliers for this title.

Touch

In this book, you will learn

- what touch is

- types of touch

- what touch tells you

3

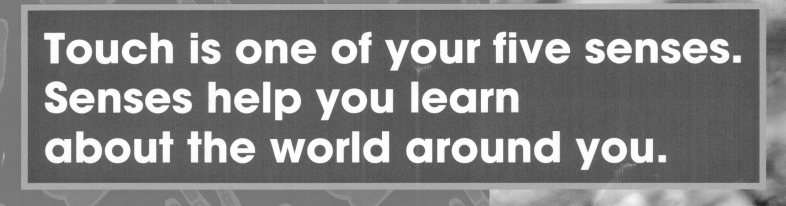

Touch is one of your five senses. Senses help you learn about the world around you.

You touch with your skin.

5

**Touch tells you
what is warm or cold.**

The Sun feels warm.

The snow feels cold.

7

Touch tells you what is rough or smooth.

The sand feels rough.

The glass feels smooth.

**Touch tells you
what is flat or wrinkly.**

A ray feels flat.

An elephant feels wrinkly.

11

Touch tells you what is dry or wet.

The dirt feels dry.

The water feels wet.

**Touch tells you
what is ticklish or prickly.**

The feathers feel ticklish.

The cactus feels prickly.

15

Touch tells you what is hard or soft.

A turtle feels hard.

A puppy feels soft.

Touch tells you what is square or round.

The blocks feel square.

The ball feels round.

If you touched this flower, how would it feel?

21

What do these things feel like?
Smooth   Rough   Dry   Wet
Wrinkly   Flat   Ticklish   Prickly

22

23

KEY WORDS

Research has shown that as much as 65 percent of all written material published in English is made up of 300 words. These 300 words cannot be taught using pictures or learned by sounding them out. They must be recognized by sight. This book contains 28 common sight words to help young readers improve their reading fluency and comprehension. This book also teaches young readers several important content words, such as proper nouns. These words are paired with pictures to aid in learning and improve understanding.

Sight Words

a	it	this
about	learn	water
an	like	what
around	of	with
do	one	world
hard	or	would
help	tells	you
how	the	your
if	these	
is	things	

Content Words

ball	flower	skin
blocks	glass	snow
cactus	puppy	Sun
dirt	ray	touch
elephant	sand	turtle
feathers	senses	

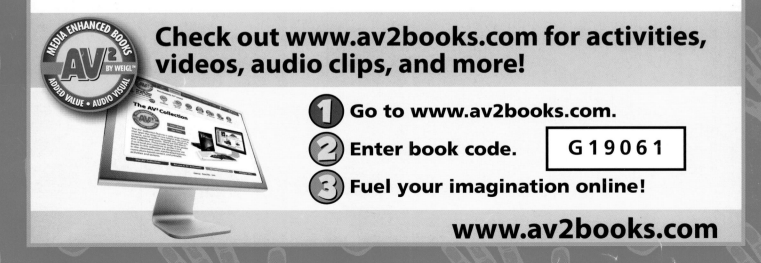

Check out www.av2books.com for activities, videos, audio clips, and more!

1 Go to www.av2books.com.

2 Enter book code. G 1 9 0 6 1

3 Fuel your imagination online!

www.av2books.com